Paris Hilton

THE NAKED TRUTH

Paris Hilton

THE NAKED TRUTH

George Mair

An "Express Paperback"
Chamberlain Bros.
a member of Penguin Group (USA) Inc.
New York

Chamberlain Bros.
a member of
Penguin Group (USA) Inc.
375 Hudson Street
New York, NY 10014

LIBRARY OF CONGRESS CATALOGING-IN-PUBLICATION DATA
Mair, George.
  Paris Hilton : the naked truth / by George Mair.
    p. cm.
  ISBN 1-59609-003-0
  1. Hilton, Paris, 1981– 2. Hilton Family. 3. Celebrities—United States—Biography.
  4. Socialites—United States—Biography. 5. Models (Persons)—United States—
  Biography. 6. Actors—United States—Biography. I. Title.
  CT275.H59926M35 2004   2004009822
  973.931'092—dc22

Printed in the United States of America

1 3 5 7 9 10 8 6 4 2

Book designed by Mike Rivilis.

CONTENTS

The One-Minute Paris Hilton

You obviously want to know more about Paris Hilton or you wouldn't have picked up this book. Just to get started, here's a one-minute thumbnail sketch, all emery-boarded and polished up, of Paris the Heiress.

Paris is one of the Hilton Hotel Hiltons, worth beaucoup bucks, an infamous party girl and a seemingly endless source of tabloid fodder. You and I may not have attended the parties she has—mostly scantily clad, sometimes even topless—but you've sure enough heard about them. Maybe you have even seen her topless in *Vanity Fair*, or costarring in Fox television's reality series *The Simple Life* with Nicole Richie, Lionel's daughter. She has had small parts in movies like *Wonderland*, *The Cat in the Hat*, and *Zoolander*. Her biggest hit to date, however, has to be the steamy tape she made with her then boyfriend, now referred to simply as The Video. (More about that later.) Paris also has a younger sister, Nicky, who was at one time part of the same party scene as Paris but now she is pursuing fashion design instead. (Just for the record, Paris and Nicky have two younger brothers, Barron and Conrad, named for their grandfather and great-grandfather respectively.) Both sisters are wildly popular in such far-flung places as Japan, where together they have made television commercials. On her own, Nicky has designed handbags for Samantha Thavasa. The Hilton sisters are so popular they can't go out in public without being mobbed. They are part of a new breed of wealthy young women on the Los Angeles-Manhattan-South Beach circuit referred to as "celebutantes." While you may harbor some preconceived notions about such creatures, especially Paris Hilton, read on and you'll be surprised to find that what you thought was true, isn't necessarily so. The common split opinion was expressed recently on E! television after it was announced that Paris was planning to record an album. While one pundit quipped that he hoped she would, and that it would become known as the worst in the history of the world, another said he sincerely wished Paris Hilton all the success in the world—that she made him proud to be an American. Go figure.

1.

The World Has Two Parts

The world can be split into two camps: those who know who the Hilton sisters are and those who don't. Those who do know of the Hiltons are split into two camps: those who are repulsed by Paris and Nicky's wealth, flagrant sexuality, and arrogance and those who are attracted by the same wealth, sexuality and arrogance.

Paris, twenty-three, and Nicky, twenty-one, were born rich—very rich! They grew up in a forty-room mansion in Los Angeles and the penthouse suite of the Waldorf-Astoria Hotel, part of the Hilton Hotel chain. As the great-granddaughters of hotel czar Conrad Hilton, the sisters have always lived in a world of nannies, doting servants, and chauffeurs on call. Beyond their enormous wealth, they also grew up to be tall, tanned, blue-eyed blond beauties whose parents introduced them to the social scene of the rich and restless while still in their teens. They were immediately the focus of the cameras of the paparazzi who were drawn to the sisters' microminiskirted luscious legs. Almost instantly, the two became the new "It" girls in Hollywood, Las Vegas, and New York—all towns dominated by hotels owned by their family.

Early on, Paris and Nicky loved the attention. And they quickly learned how to draw the attention of men. She has no problem baring her own medium-sized breasts freely and frequently everywhere from the pages of *Vanity Fair* to frolics in swimming pools to forays to Vegas strip joints. One explanation might be that despite all her material advantages, she lacks taste, class, and ultimately, self-respect. One has to wonder why she was raised that way. For all intents and purposes, the Hilton sisters just want to enjoy life. Dismissing those who criticize them, Paris said, "People love to hate us. But when you know us, you love us."

In Paris Hilton's mind, she is a victim of circumstances beyond her control. She says it is not her fault that she is rich and beautiful and wooed by men. "It's not my fault—why be mad at me?" This is a question that beggars belief after the release of her explicit video. Despite the embarrassment, the hand-wringing, and the lawsuits following that little caper, Paris has done little to tone down her scintillating lifestyle.

Paris has a chunk of a family fortune worth about $300 million and still she just wants people to like her. It bothers her, in fact, that people whisper about her wherever she goes. Respect and admiration don't automatically go with money, however. It's doubtful that her great-grandfather Conrad, who founded his empire in Texas, would approve of Paris's behavior today, just like he didn't approve of his son Barron's behavior years ago. While Paris's two brothers are not an intimate part of her life, her father, Rick, and her mother, Kathy [Richards], are. Kathy, a former child star, is in constant contact with her daughters. In a declaration of liberty, Paris told one interviewer: "I've been working hard, and I'm not trying to live off my name. I'm recording an album, I'm acting in movies. And I've done it all on my own. I don't want to run hotels, I want to make my own name for myself."

Surprisingly, Hollywood is actually taking Paris seriously, and she is appearing in *Raising Helen*, along with Kate Hudson, in 2005, and *Win a Date with Tad Hamilton*. She is taking acting classes along with other aspiring actresses. In a stab at sincerity, Paris makes the point that she doesn't need the money. She just wants to be accepted as a professional actress, just like her mother was years ago. It's rumored that she is being besieged with offers, but that may just be talk. Part of her taking her career seriously is seen in her buying a house in West Hollywood with Nicky so she can be closer to the studios and buying her own car—admittedly, not just any car but a Mercedes convertible—so she can go out on auditions more easily. All of which she shares with Tinkerbell, her ever-present Chihuahua she is often seen carrying, and a bulldog named Max.

Paris, who was nicknamed "Star" by her family when she was a little girl, has already appeared in *The Simple Life*, a so-called real-life version of the 1960s television series *Green Acres*. And the premise of the show is indeed a simple one: two city girls move to a small family farm in the small town of Altus, Arkansas, population 817. They performed all the usual chores, including milking cows, making their beds, and flipping burgers at the local fast food restaurant. This led to Paris's astounding discovery that people actually had to work for a living. Towards the end of the show, Paris seemed to appreciate the time she had spent in Altus, and understand the reward of a hard day's work.

Paris is our modern-day
version of a debutante.
Why bother with a coming-out
party when she's out partying
all the time already?

2.

The Beginning of Paris Hilton

The dizzing ride began twenty-three years ago when Paris was born to Rick and Kathy Hilton on February 17, 1981. Almost from the beginning, she would never be known as just Paris Hilton: she was "Paris Hilton, great-granddaughter of Conrad Hilton, founder of the Hilton Hotels" or "Paris the Heiress" and on and on. Other notable women in the Hilton family who were not overshadowed by the name include Elizabeth Taylor, who for a short time was the first wife of Paris's grandfather Conrad "Nicky" Hilton, Jr., before divorcing him because of "irreconcilable differences" and leaving with a $24 million settlement, and Zsa Zsa Gabor, second wife of Paris's great-grandfather, the devout Catholic founder of the Hilton empire. With her younger sister Nicky, born in 1983, Paris has every intention of outgrowing the name.

Paris grew up at one of the fanciest addresses in Manhattan, the

Waldorf-Astoria, as well as in Beverly Hills and the Hamptons. After being done with school (or school being done with her) she and her family decided that her next institution of higher learning would not be college but the world of high society. By the year 2000 she was working on an advanced degree in being famous. "We would go to parties. Before long, we were made out by the media just to be party girls." Even though she and Nicky were having fun, they were also networking and making contacts to promote their modeling and acting careers. Paris proudly says she makes her own money and pays her own way, adding, "I know that I'm pretty, but that just means I have to work even harder."

Paris first learned to model, appearing in fashion shows for designers Marc Bouwer and Catherine Malandrino. In time she signed on to do an advertising layout for the Italian label Iceberg. She was getting noticed, getting invited to high-octane parties, getting into magazines like *GQ*, *Vanity Fair*, and *FHM*. Often, she was with Nicky, and as they became the talk of the fashion and party circuits they became famous, as detractors jabbed, simply for being famous. This image was only enhanced when a profile of the two appeared in *People* magazine.

Paris has worked hard training to be a professional model. Lesser souls may not understand, but the key to modeling success is the walk. All of us know how to walk, but knowing how to walk down a catwalk is another matter altogether. The trick is to swing one leg seductively ahead of the other to the beat of the music, and to learn how to do it right Paris went to the most renown expert in the field, "the Walking Man," Willi Ninja, made famous in the 1990s documentary named, no kidding, *Paris Is Burning*. He taught her her special catwalk strut.

At one time, girls in Hilton's social class would have been destined to be debutantes, then wives. Paris is our modern-day version of a debutante. Why bother with a coming-out party when she's out partying all the time already?

The Hilton family has not needed help climbing the social ladder. Paris is already at the top.

3.

Tugs in All Directions

A beautiful rich girl gets pulled in so many different directions. Tugs from parents, from peers, from the media, and a combination of subtle and in-your-face prejudices can muddle a teenager's thinking no matter what her home life or family fortune's may be. Nowhere are values more confused than in New York City, the stratosphere of wealth and social position where forces converge and diverge in ways that are perceptible only to those involved. Put the handful of acceptable private schools in Manhattan, Brooklyn, Queens, and the Bronx under the microscope and you get a window into the thinking not only of the students enrolled in them but even more into the thinking of their parents.

Take Dwight, the posh coed school Paris attended. It's known throughout the prep school milieu by the spelled-out put-down acronym taken from its name: "Dumb White Idiots Getting High Together." All the elite schools have their own distinct personalities, just as their counterpart colleges do. Tuition runs into the tens of thousands of dollars per year, and the wealthy vie contentiously to snap an acceptance for their precious offspring.

Brearley girls have the reputation of being so serious and so involved in their studies that they are labeled unfeminine by some of the city's more style-conscious rich. A typical Brearley student may be long on academics, they observe, but short on personal appearance. The parents may be hippies, and one mother noted with raised eyebrow that some Brearley fathers even sport beards. "I don't think I'd want my daughter to go there," she added. According to an article in *W* magazine, in fact, Brearley girls lately look to Janet Reno as a role model. Yet Diana Vreeland, Helen Frankenthaler, and Doris Duke all are counted among alumnae.

Chapin is considered by many to be the most social of the schools—social as in old money rather than new. Jacqueline Bouvier attended Chapin, as did Lily Pulitzer and Aurin Lauder, and more recently the children of Tom Wolfe and Kathleen Turner. Chapin students are supposedly oblivious to the paparazzi. One of Chapin's more cherished traditions, in fact, is handbell concerts, not your average high school activity.

Money is not a high priority for students at Collegiate; it's not discussed because it's just there, always has been, always will be. John Kennedy, Jr., was an alumnus, and his sister, Caroline Kennedy Schlossberg, and Steve Kroft have sent their children there.

Gweneth Paltrow and Jade Jagger attended Spence, considered by many to be the school for the richest of the rich. One mother commented that it would be hard to keep her children's feet on the ground if they studied biology and history alongside the offspring of billionaires at Spence.

It's not unusual for couples to start lobbying to get their child in one of these schools as soon as the pregnancy test comes back positive. But even that kind of effort, as well as a family legacy at a given school, does not guarantee placement. Why's that? One factor is the rarely publicly discussed Prep for Prep scholarship program. Prep for Prep affords deserving children of color a chance at the good life while adding some needed diversity to the student body at the same time. But Prep for Prep also takes away coveted seats from the old guard, and Prep for Prep students often walk away with the top honors at graduation. The mix has caused chinks in the long-standing armor-plated old money network, with students scattered among schools other than those of their parents' first choosing and some even finding their way into the so-called Jewish schools. JAP used to stand for "Jewish American Princess," but now it's lost its religious and gender overtones to refer to prep school students generally. Chevy Chase, Sean Lennon, and Claire Danes all went to Dalton. And, according to Goldman, even when parents do get their little ones into Episcopal, they are already gritting their teeth about getting them into Buckley or Chapin.

While Prep for Prep students don't have the kind of money to throw around that their classmates do, they may be responsible for improving their classmates' study habits. You can see this in one of today's hottest trends among the rich: hiring a tutor to help prepare for the SAT. Arun Alagappan, the director of Advantage Testing, is said to charge $565 per session for his services, worth every penny to those looking to beat out the competition and get into their Ivy League college of choice.

Then there is the prep school competition at the material level—

what's "in" and what's "over"—especially for girls. The right Prada bag, for instance, or the designer jeans of the moment are as distinctive as badges of honor as tattoos are for gangs. Shopping is an art form for these girls, learned so well from their style-conscious mothers. Yet the superficiality of their affluent lifestyle, ironically, may be no better than that of the less affluent girl who haunts to local mall, the difference being the brands—Gucci, Dior, Armani, Tiffany, Cartier—and the cost—a week on Maui in some cases. "You need to dress the way you want to be perceived," a Spence girl intoned. The look at her school, at last check, was WASPy and subtle, with tennis shoes in and heels out. But that could change any minute, like a flock of birds making an unexpected U-turn mid-flight. At schools like Chapin, Nightingale, and Sacred Heart, where uniforms are required, a given clique is identified by bag, shoe, or jewelry alone. It's not unusual, for instance, to see a clutch of girls all clutching identical Prada bags.

Girls enrolled in all-girl schools often find themselves dateless because there are not enough eligible boys for them to go out with. At the coed schools, students date each other. It's little wonder that the all-girl students do whatever they can to get noticed by boys, like hiking their skirts way up or wearing barely there shoes. The headmistress at Spence supposedly marks the thighs and heels of her overexposed charges with an indelible pen so that only long enough skirts and "real" shoes will cover the lines of demarcation. Some girls actually choose not to be part of any clique, however, which thrills some mothers but has others chewing their nails to the quick fearing that, down the line, the right marriage won't be contracted if their daughters aren't part of the game.

The use of drugs and alcohol by hormone-revved teens concerns parents and schools everywhere, and the weekend lives of some prep school kids would upset any adult. With money being no concern, marijuana and cocaine are delivered to Park Avenue parties while parents are out on the town. However, the scene today is milder than it was a few years ago when raves flourished in warehouses all over town. One girl recalls the jars of free Ecstasy at the door. And while a few students still get blazed on coke, the latest things are late-night pubs and Chinese restaurants where management averts their eyes to underage patrons. Even fourteen-year-olds are out on the town, hanging out on street corners on Friday night. Yet Michael Heller, a young entrepreneur who runs Park Avenue Entertainment, claims that IDs are checked more thoroughly than ever at the newer clubs, such as Spa, and even really well-made fakes are getting spotted and underaged patrons turned away.

A young woman who attended Nightingale recalled that marijuana surpassed tobacco when she was there, and that senior year all of the kids were so relieved to get accepted into college that they spent most of the spring partying. Cigarettes are still popular enough that there is a courtyard in an apartment building that is a known gathering place for lunchtime smokers from Dalton, Spence, Sacred Heart, Nightingale, Trevor Day, and St. David's schools.

Despite the peer pressure to party, there is an underlying level of seriousness to maintain the chances of getting into Ivy league schools. Never before have there been so many applicants to the top colleges and universities. My dad would kill me if I got into trouble," a Spence girl said, confiding she has taken up smoking, drinking beer, and smoking marijuana occasionally. "He thinks I have to go to Yale."

Kat Cohen, the director of Ivywise, a college counseling service, said there has been a 69 percent increase in college applications from the girls' schools. She believes girls today have a greater sense of personal responsibility than they did a few years ago, they put more pressure on themselves to succeed. Again, this trend may be due to the Prep for Prep students.

Schools like Spence are still bastions of old money, and, as another observer explained, the students are divided into two groups: those who have always had money and those wish that they had always had money. When a child does not get into the school the parents have chosen, the envy and hatred for those who did is almost palpable, a sentiment that is often passed on to the children. One uniquely city phenomenon is the play date, an unusual form of social climbing wherein the little kindergartener learns to be a lifelong snoop. Here's how it works: A mother wishing to move up the social ladder makes a play date for her daughter with the daughter of a mother she envies. After the first date, the envious mother quizzes her daughter about envied mother's apartment: the size, the layout, the number of servants, and so on. Ideally, the girls get along famously, and pretty soon the envious mother is picking up her daughter at the envied mother's apartment instead of having the nanny do it. Before long, the mothers "do" lunch, then there's a dinner party where the husbands meet, and, voila, a whole new world opens up to the couple, let alone their unwitting daughter. The interesting yet sad thing is, most of these children then grow up accepting this type of phoniness with a smirk. They know it's a ridiculous game yet they also enjoy being part of it. And, in turn, they no doubt will pass it on to their children. Of course, the Hilton family has not needed help climbing the social ladder. Paris is already at the top.

4.

Famous for Being Famous

There are a lot of people who don't like Paris Hilton or her sister Nicky. Or, for that matter, their mother Kathy, although she is not so irritatingly visible on the party scene as her daughters are. These people feel Paris is just too too: too young, too pretty, too rich, too cutesy. But the most damning criticism of all leveled against Paris is that she has no class, and for the power elite of Manhattan's Upper East Side, nothing could be worse.

The no class reputation comes from Paris's mindless excesses that leave gossip columnists and paparazzi alike drooling: the partying, the breast baring, the almost pathetic hunger for recognition. This last indictment comes from the semi-pleading, almost angry question she is known to pose to party guests, waiters, or assorted bystanders depending on the occasion: "Don't you know who I am?" Mostly, they do. And, mostly, they don't give a damn.

For example, Paris's arrogance erupted when she got into a scrape with a Las Vegas stripper who was flirting with her date. Why such a pretty, rich girl would care about a stripper is beyond almost anyone's understanding. Why someone would be in a strip joint with a date in tow is almost beyond comprehension. On the night in question, Paris was admonished by club security to quiet down. This only gave her license to trump her two previous gaffes with a third: she started yelling that it was her grandfather who built Las Vegas in the first place. Not entirely true, of course, and no doubt Barron Hilton would be less than thrilled to know his granddaughter was making a scene in such an establishment.

And what's with that name? What kind of name is Paris anyway? Again, it is just too cute. And what does it mean in the greater Hilton scheme of things? In some ways, "Cisco" would have been more apt, the name of the town in Texas where Conrad Hilton bought his first hotel in 1919 and launched the fortune than eventually launched Paris. There may be a bit of Conrad and Barron in Paris, too. Conrad was a womanizer with a taste for showgirls; his son Nicky had similar taste, marrying an eighteen-year-old Elizabeth Taylor only to be shamed when she filed for divorce accusing him of beating her. In many people's minds, it was Conrad who disgraced the Hilton name the most when divorced, he married Zsa Zsa Gabor. The Catholic Church denied him the sacrament of Holy Communion for that transgression, a very grievous thing to him, but it didn't keep him from chasing after women. Some feel that his leaving most of his estate to the church and not his family was his way of doing penance for marrying Zsa Zsa.

Then there are the whispers about how Paris couldn't have posed for *Vanity Fair* clad only in a necklace without her parents being in on it. What kind of parents are Rick and Kathy Hilton to let Paris behave this way? "They have all the decorum of trailer trash who have just won the lottery," one Manhattanite opines. "They make money look cheap."

But not everybody agrees. Donald Trump, who owns the T Management Modeling Agency that first signed Paris and landed her a contract with Iceberg jeans, is a Paris supporter. Even if many of the old guard don't like her, there are many more who do and are willing to put up with Paris's shenanigans.

Some people feel that no one has worked harder at being famous without actually achieving anything than Paris and Nicky Hilton. The sisters are ridiculed for attending so many parties or appearing at so many Hollywood events. But this criticism is not entirely fair, since Paris has already had her own television series and has appeared in movies while Nicky's designs have sold so well in Japan and other designs are coming down the pike. True, for a long time it seemed that all they did was go to the beauty salon, but that's all changed.

And then, of course, the Hilton sisters serve another purpose than many don't recognize: they are barometers of what is meaningful and important in our society today. As media darlings, their every exploit is reported in newspapers, magazines, and on television. Paris and Nicky garner more television time, in fact, than any president, Supreme Court justice, legislator, or all the intellectuals in universities across America combined. This fact tells us something about ourselves: we are obsessed with people who are famous, and not just those who act, sing, play sports, and engage in politics. Fame can come from scandal, a reality show, a website. Paris has been involved in all three. Soon she'll have an album recorded, and maybe a self-titled book or PlayStation game named after her.

It was the Fox network, after all, that used Paris then inexplicable fame to promote *The Simple Life* to such Nielsen success. The astonishing truth revealed there is that people can become famous for no real reason.

Real or not, the public's insatiable appetite for fame wins viewers for news and entertainment features alike. When anything happens, producers scramble for some "expert" to expound on anything from exploding mayonnaise jars in Java to heliotropic skin divers in Portugal to liven up the news and give the pretty boy anchor who can barely tie a Windsor knot something to talk about. Exaggerated? Yes, but not much—just keep watching.

It all comes down to feeding public curiosity, a demand so strong that even the most marginal celebrity can become the focus of national attention.

As Rich Hanley, director of graduate programs at Connecticut's Quinnipiac University's school of communication, says, "Paris Hilton is famous simply because she is famous. That's it. She can be interpreted, in fact, as the ultimate postmodern celebrity." Hanley adds that Paris has essentially done nothing, not even anything all that silly, unless you want to count stepping in a fishpond or falling off a horse or making a racy video. Yet "[s]he is a global celebrity," he goes on, "celebrated simply for being, well, celebrated, and for drinking with celebrities who might actually have done something measurable." People like Paris act as filler, to occupy all the time between events that really mean something. Or as Anthony Mora, who wrote *Spin to Win*, a primer for becoming famous through the media, sums up about the Hiltons having worked so hard to become famous for nothing, "It takes a lot of time and effort to get all this attention without having done anything."

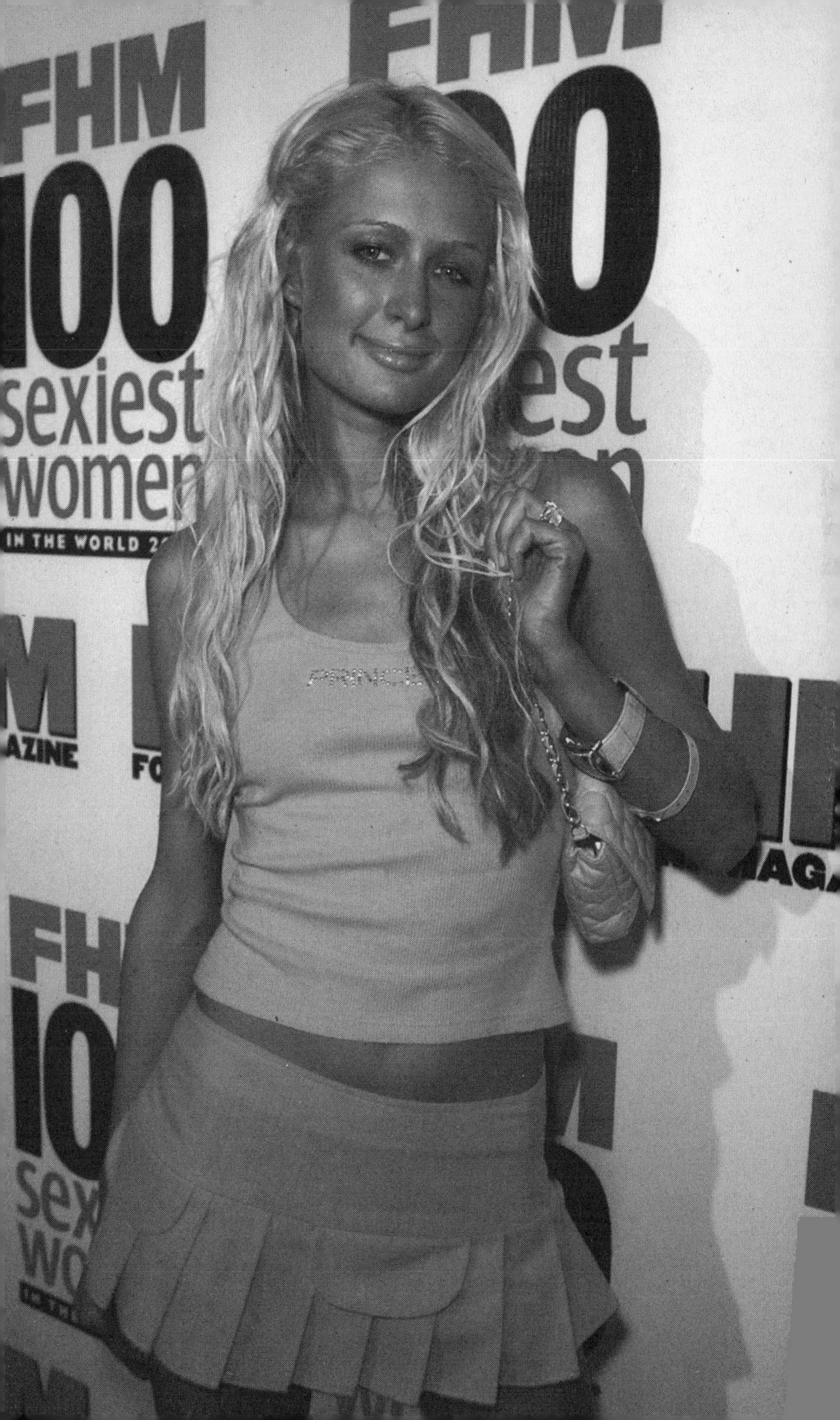
FHM
100
sexiest
women

5.

The Paris Buzz:
Who Makes It and Why?

What is the story with the video? Shot in 2000 in a hotel room in Las Vegas, it shows Paris having sex with her then-boyfriend, Rick Salomon. That isn't the big deal. The big deal is that it surfaced on the Internet, and that it was being offered on eBay, along with a T-shirt reading: I'VE SEEN PARIS. As liberal as Paris's parents may be, they were furious, and issued the following statement, as reported in the *New York Post*: "Anyone in any way involved in this video is guilty of criminal activity, and will be . . . vigorously prosecuted." Not to be left out of the loop, the ex-boyfriend raced to file a slander suit against Paris, her parents, and her publicist. Bent out of shape, he contended that the Hiltons were out to get him—depicting him as a bad guy and even a rapist. It was a malicious move to shield her reputation, he charged. The Hiltons snapped back that he was lying.

Most of the public wanted to know what the problem was. Isn't Paris always falling out of her dress in public, baring her breasts, teasing people's fantasies? Haven't she and Nicky been flaunting themselves as the newest party girls? So what image is it, exactly, that she and her family are so anxious to protect?

Robert Thompson, professor of pop culture at Syracuse University, says part of the problem is the growing demand for titillation not only from the public but from the media itself. "When there were only three TV channels, you could only use so much celebrity, but now you have to cast the net much wider. . . . We watch them as we scratch our heads and wonder how they ever got to where they are."

None of the Hiltons' escapades are "accidental," claims Betsy Rott, vice president of original program for the E! network, which first aired a biography of the Hiltons in March 2003. She believes the public fascination with the sisters comes from an unspoken agreement between the media and the sisters themselves. Essentially, it goes: Tell us where your cameras will be and we'll guarantee we'll be there in fishnet stocking and no bra, with Tinkerbell, the Chihuahua, in tow. "These girls would go out at night and work it," said Rott. "They knew where the paparazzi were, and they would pose. They are just what the gossip columns and the paparazzi need to have and the women [the Hiltons] love it. They get hooked on the glamour and the attention. It was addictive. They got to be celebrities without having to do anything."

Even more pointedly, Paris and Nicky are favorites of Richard Johnson, editor of the *New York Post*'s Page Six. His explanation is simple and straightforward: "They are pretty, rich, and fun. Paris loves the camera. . . . I imagine when when she's old, ugly, and poor, people will lose interest, but she has a long run yet." And Michelle Lee, author of *Fashion Victim: Our Love-Hate Relationship With Dressing, Shopping, and the Cost of Style*, says there's something magnetic about Paris: "I think she's beautiful. Part of the reason is the aura of scandal around her. You know, she's sort of a bad girl." While Simon Doonan, the acerbic creative director of Barneys New York and *New York Observer* columnist, adds that the Hilton sisters are part rich heiress and part trailer park trash and that fascinates people.

On the other side of the coin, Bryan Rabin, a party planner based in Los Angeles, thinks that the sisters' behavior is condoned, even encouraged, by their parents, which he finds exploitative and despicable. Betsy Rott thinks that while Nicky could develop into a credible fashion designer, Paris will give acting a shot for a while and then get on the marriage-divorce treadmill, just like Elizabeth Taylor and Zsa Zsa Gabor did before her, thus cementing a quasi-psychic connection with Hilton family karma. And although nobody has been listening, Paris herself has been talking about marriage and babies already, purring about having a daughter of her own in the next few years. But what will she call her? London? Bangkok? D.C.? Fresno? Cast your vote now!

Conrad Hilton's devotion to the Catholic Church, and Saint Joseph in particular, paid off again when one Sunday morning at mass he spotted a beautiful woman wearing a red hat.

6.

Hilton Family History and Where the Money Came From

Two men who had a profound impact on the life that Paris Hilton leads today are her great-grandfather, Conrad Nicholson Hilton, and her grandfather, Barron Hilton. Conrad Hilton made the family enormously rich on paper but didn't believe in leaving any money to his heirs. Barron Hilton didn't give a damn what his father thought and circumvented the old man's will and made not only himself rich but his descendents as well, including Paris. If Conrad's will had remained as he left it, Paris today might be asking, "Would you like fries with that?"

Conrad was a very religious man who in the last forty years of his life rarely missed Sunday mass. He enlisted in the Army in World War I and planned to join his father as a partner in a grocery store when he got out, even though he really was intrigued with banking. But Conrad's father was killed in a car accident just before the war ended, so once Conrad was a civilian again, he began looking around the New Mexico Territory and Texas for a bank to buy. He had $5,000 in savings. One day, his wanderings brought him to the tiny boomtown of Cisco, Texas, with its swarms of oilmen clamoring for lodging and the only hotel in town renting rooms on three eight-hour shifts. He was too late to get a room, and had to wait eight hours until the next shift of rooms became available. There was already a line of men waiting.

Conrad Hilton immediately understood. Here was a booming business, renting rooms for eight hours at a time, and there was a constant stream of customers eager for the rooms three times a day, day after day. It didn't take a rocket scientist to figure out that the hotel business would be a cash cow, and on an impulse Conrad asked the owner if the hotel, the Mobley, was for sale. Surprisingly, the owner said it was. He wanted to get out of the business. The price: $50,000. With only a week to raise the money, Conrad consulted to two guiding lights in his life—his mother and Saint Joseph—and decided to go ahead. With a $5,000 deposit pinned to the inside of his coat, he set about contacting friends as well as the local bank to borrow the rest. It was all coming together just fine until the day before the deadline when one friend's check bounced and it looked like the whole deal would fall through. Conrad again prayed to Saint Joseph, then again went to see the banker to try to convince him to save the deal by loaning $5,000 to the friend whose check had bounced. Miraculously, the banker agreed, the deal was finalized, and Conrad Hilton was in the hotel business. The year was 1919.

Skating on thin ice right up to the last minute would become the story of Conrad Hilton's life. The Waldorf-Astoria, the grandest hotel of them all and the ultimate dream for a hotelman, was bought this way. In that deal, Hilton thought he had all the money in hand and was within an hour of closing when all of a sudden a partner withdrew, leaving Hilton not $5,000 short but $500,000! Astonishingly, he managed to come up with the half million in under ten minutes.

Back at the Mobley, Conrad came up with two concepts that would become the key to his enormous success in the hotel business in the years to come. First, he told his staff that they were the Mobley Hotel and not he. He rarely saw the guests, but the bellboys, clerks, chamber maids, and other staff saw guests all the time. He insisted that they be friendly, courteous, and keep the hotel as clean and appealing as possible. Second, he wanted to emphasize what was profitable and eliminate what wasn't. While the Mobley renting rooms for eight-hour shifts made money because there were no other hotels around, the dining didn't because there were other places to eat nearby. The dining room's profits per square foot were nothing compared to the rooms' square footage returns. So, he closed the dining room, built partitions to create more rooms, and immediately improved his bottom line. It was this type of thinking that made him one of the most successful hotelmen in history, ultimately heading a billion-dollar empire with hundreds of hotels that included the fabled Waldorf-Astoria as its crown jewel. Along the way, he became friends with presidents, movie stars, sports heroes, and other notables. He never stopped thanking his mother or Saint Joseph for his good fortune.

Conrad Hilton's father, a Norwegian immigrant, and his mother, a German American, imbued him with the American dream. He was devoted to his mother, always maintaining that any strength he had over the years was due to her, as well as his belief in God, his belief in the brotherhood of man, and his belief in his country. He believed that it was God's plan that we help those who are less fortunate than ourselves. But these beliefs, so dear to Conrad, were not shared by his children or their children.

Conrad Hilton's devotion to the Catholic Church, and Saint Joseph in particular, paid off again when one Sunday morning at mass he spotted a beautiful woman wearing a red hat. Her name was Mary Barron and a mutual friend eventually introduced them. They soon married, and their union produced three boys: Conrad Jr., William Barron, and Eric Michael. Mary and Conrad divorced in 1934.

In 1942, Conrad married actress Zsa Zsa Gabor, whom he called "Georgia" because he couldn't pronounce her name. Five years later they were divorced, and soon after she bore him a daughter, Francesca. Zsa Zsa made a career out of getting married—she did it eleven times in all—starting at the tender age of fifteen. Her shortest marriage, to Felipe de Alba, lasted an impulsive one day; director John Huston joked at the time that he hadn't even give it that long. At least the marriage to Conrad lasted five years. It all began when Conrad ran into Zsa Zsa at the fabled Ciro's restaurant in Hollywood, where she was having dinner with Beverly Hills hotshot lawyer Greg Bautzer. Her first impression of Hilton was that he was a six-foot-two cowboy right out of the American west. When he danced with her, he held her so tight she could barely breathe, yet all the while she was thinking: "I'm going to marry this man, this

Conrad Hilton." He offered her $20,000 right there if she would fly with him to Miami Beach, but, smart about the ways of men, Zsa Zsa knew if she accepted he would think he could always have his way. They did get married four months later, in a civil ceremony in Santa Fe, New Mexico. Conrad played the domineering master, but she held her own in the relationship and he loved her for it. She was all of seventeen years old at the time and he was sixty-one.

Two things cast a pall over the marriage. As a divorced man, Conrad could no longer receive communion in the Catholic Church. With Zsa Zsa broadcasting that he was "a wonderful lover, virile, well-endowed, and masterful," obviously relishing the sex she was having with him, he may have felt even more guilty. Yet enjoy Zsa Zsa as he might, and guilty as he felt, he still was not above flirting with other women, all the while demanding that Zsa Zsa be at his beck and call. She did get him to get rid of the cowboy boots and hat and dress more stylishly. After all, Zsa Zsa was used to moving in rarified circles with the likes of Howard Hughes, Errol Flynn, and William Paley pawing over her before she ever met Hilton.

Zsa Zsa's assessment of Conrad Hilton was that money was his god, that the Catholic Church and, shockingly, white supremacy were his religion. In her book *One Lifetime Is Not Enough*, she writes: "He always struck me as having Nazi tendencies—especially in later years when I discovered that one of his most trusted employees was a former Gauleiter and once or twice made the terrible faux pas of introducing him to someone as, 'My husband, Conrad Hitler.' Conrad laughed uproariously which I found chilling."

Perhaps one of the surprising—or, maybe, not so surprising—aspects of Zsa Zsa Gabor's time as a Hilton wife was toward the end of the marriage when another man entered her life. This other man was none other than her stepson Conrad Jr., nicknamed "Nicky." She and Nicky were much closer in age than she and Conrad. Conrad knew all about the affair, but was either too proud or too hurt to admit it. He would later comment that Zsa Zsa brought him not only laughter and gaiety but also headaches and heartaches. Conrad later blamed the breakup on Zsa Zsa, saying his marriage to her, a divorcee, separated him from his church.

The affair between Zsa Zsa and Nicky lasted into her marriage to George Sanders and Nicky's marriage in 1950 to Elizabeth Taylor—his moment of glory and then shame when she quickly divorced him. He didn't spend their wedding night with her, he drank, he gambled, he beat her. Nicky's short marriage to Taylor cost the Hiltons millions. Nicky tragically died of a heart attack in February 1969 at the age of forty-two. Zsa Zsa's final assessment: he knew he could never live up to his father's example, but he was damned to live forever in his father's shadow.

Conrad Hilton originally wanted his son Barron to start at the bottom of the Hilton organization and work his way up, but Barron didn't like that idea, saying the pay was too low. He eventually dabbled in a number of other things. During World War II, he enlisted as a photographer in the Navy, after which he first bought an orange juice business in Southern California, and then an aviation leasing business, before he finally buckled and joined the family business in 1951. As a side interest, Barron started up the San Diego Chargers football team in 1960. In 1966 he assumed the presidency of the Hilton Hotel chain. At the same time, he also started spending a lot of time at his ranch in Nevada. "I do a lot of fishing, hunting and flying. I've got a helicopter, some airplanes and balloons."

While Barron Hilton bumbled several major projects during his tenure, he did two things that have made Paris and the rest of the family quite happy. First, in 1970 he got Hilton Hotels into the gambling business and today their casinos dominate the action in Las Vegas, pulling in lots of money. Second, in 1979 he fought to repeal his father's will.

Conrad Hilton didn't believe in inherited wealth, earmarking most of his fortune for the Catholic Church and other charities, but his children, led by Barron, were left with little and decided to take the will to court. Barron had a clever lawyer and won, in 1988. His net worth jumped to $335 million overnight. His stepsister Francesca, on the other hand, didn't have a good lawyer, and she lost her case and was disinherited, no doubt leaving her the poorest Hilton in town. The key was that Barron didn't contest the trust his father had set up with the church and the charities but instead argued that he should administer it. Part of the fortune still went to the church, just as Conrad had intended, but most went to Barron and his descendents, including the lovely Paris. Ironically, some of the money the morally upright Conrad left to the church probably later helped pay off the many victims of sexual abuse by priests in the Los Angeles diocese.

Many observers saw the move to contest the will as lawyer-engineered flimflam, leaving the Hiltons rich but not looking good. The real villains, though, were probably the lawyers, who walked away with millions in fees that would have otherwise gone to charity. History has it that Conrad is responsible for the fortune the Hiltons enjoy today, but it's really Barron who made it all possible. Without him, Paris might be broke today. During the thirty years he was boss he was involved in several major goof-ups, such as screwing up the Hilton Hotels credit card operation. An avid poker player, he later redeemed himself when he convinced his father that the future of the hotel business was not in rooms but in gambling. They immediately got into the gaming businesss and it is still making big money for them to this day. Most of the Hilton money comes from Park Place Entertainment Corporation, the casino spin-off, which Barron still keeps a very close eye on. That's something that Paris might want to start keeping a close eye on herself one of these days.

7.

That Video

Paris Hilton and her boyfriend at the time, Rick Salomon, really fumbled with this caper. If you don't want to leave a record behind of what you did, don't make a videotape of it. But there's more to this story than just making the tape. It was stupid, but also funny and maybe even a plus for Paris. The tape ended up affecting people in all kinds of ways.

The videotape in question is twenty-seven grainy minutes of two naked people having sex. Nineteen at the time, Paris is busy showing how adorably sexy she is, cavorting around, yet also trying to seem more mature, more skilled sexually than she really is. She postures amusingly, displaying her breasts in the mirror in the bathroom where the lighting is best, hoping to entice Salomon even more. Salomon, for his part, can't keep an erection as arduously as he'd like. Paris's performance skids a bit, however, when she answers the phone in the middle of everything—her brief, monosyllabic conversation failing to reveal who is on the other end (Nicky? Mom? Room service?). This indifferent gesture couldn't have helped poor Rick's performance any too well.

Three years after the fact, the tape surfaced and immediately hit the Internet. And then, on news programs around the world, it preempted the war in Iraq, the stock market's closing bell, innumerable epidemics, strange new discoveries on Mars, and the previous night's baseball scores. How could the world possibly go on without knowing all the poop on Paris and Rick?

For example, the sober *New York Times* assigned a reporter to view the tape, no doubt awarding him hazard pay in the deal, and he was stunned that there actually was sex on the tape. The reporter supposedly watched most of the video peeking between the fingers of his hands covering his face.

In the days that followed, snickering, tsk-tsking, finger-wagging, and righteous indignation swept the country, while gossips and pundits alike had more fun than a kid with an E ticket at Disneyland. But some people didn't react that way, and, smartly, Choire Sicha, whose Gawker site first unleashed the video on the public, laid low lest he become the target of a lawsuit. He knew that the first person a rich girl like Paris turns to when she really feels wronged is not her confessor but her tough, high-octane lawyer. The fact is, most people kept their reactions to themselves, at least in public.

The Hiltons did hire public relations guru Dan Klores to put a lid on it. He immediately ordered Paris, who was returning to the United States from Australia where she had been promoting *The Simple Life*, to indeed adopt the simple life: no public appearances, no posing, no parties, no scandals. It was worse than being sent to prison. Meanwhile, Klores was all golly, gee, shucks, what's all the fuss about? The video was "inconsequential to everything that's going on in the world and it's not really even interesting sex," he told the *New York Observer*, adding that "[i]t seems like a particularly dour time in our culture. There will be outlets that want to keep it alive." In other words, the media are no better than tabloid scandalmongers. And then Klores had Paris release a smoothly written apology that characterized the whole incident as a terrible mistake that unfairly tainted her whole circle of family and friends. "I feel embarrassed and humiliated," she stated, "especially because my parents and the people who love me have been hurt. I was in an intimate relationship and never, ever thought these things would become public." Finally, Klores had Paris's saddened, loving father Rick rush onto the field of battle: "I love my daughter. It goes without saying that I was severely unhappy when I heard about this tape. I will, however, do everything I can to support my daughter in every way possible." After this first volley, Paris again withdrew from public scrutiny.

By this time, Rick Salomon had consulted a lawyer and found that he could be in jeopardy both legally and financially. But it could all just be talk, too, because what use is a client who just sits there and does nothing? First he needed to deny he did anything. And so he did. "Are you sure that's me on the tape?" he asked. From there it evolved into, Well, it was my roommate who stole the tape and sold it to a Seattle porn merchant—sort of a, Well, yes, I was there, but I didn't do it kind of defense.

Then, taking a more aggressive stance, Salomon sued the Hiltons for $10 million. On what grounds? It was for saying naughty things about him. The Hiltons were blaming him for the whole mess, he said, that he had forced Paris into having sex, no doubt a surprise to the millions worldwide who saw the tape. But people would buy the Hiltons' story just because they are the Hiltons. It was all a move to take the spotlight off Paris and put it on him. No, really?

Next on Rick Salomon's lawsuit hit parade was a claim against the Internet company, Marvad Corporation, yet again for $10 million, for peddling the tape without his permission and without paying royalties. Marvad countersued Rick's roommate, Don Thrasher, also for $10 million, for selling the video. (Numerically speaking, it seems the $10 million key was the only one working on any number of litigious keyboards.)

In the end, what was the impact of all this silly blather? First off, most people saw it all as less a morality play and more a business ploy. Cynical as it sounds, Paris Hilton clearly made herself the center of attention once again. All the provocative clothing, all the dancing on tabletops, all the baring of breasts, the photo spreads in *Vanity Fair*, the petulant Don't you know who I am?—she duped the media into making her famous. But the video, three years in the can, doesn't seem to have been part of that plan. She didn't really need the publicity. Serious observers think the video may hurt Paris's acting career in the long run, perhaps dooming her to be typecast in sex kitten roles— roles that quickly loose their believability and therefore marketability past the mid to late twenties, only a couple of years away for Paris.

In the short run, the scandal benefited people like Rupert Murdock, who owns Fox, the network that carried *The Simple Life*. And next season? If Paris can't deliver, Murdock can always get a newer, younger face that can.

One thing the video did produce was an avalanche of words. Everybody had an opinion, everybody felt free to snicker, snipe, and scold. The *New York Observer* reviewed the tape in almost serious tones: "In her debut as an adult-film actress, Paris Hilton offers a taste of good things to come." They noted that neither the camera nor Mr. Salomon's penis functioned properly. Paris was described as "playful," with a "gamine" personality well suited to the genre. It was the reviewer's sincere hope that she would not be distracted away from this, her true calling, where her true talents obviously lie, by doing a mere television series. It was a good start in the adult film business for Paris, he concluded.

Crisis Management 101

There are many ways to handle image problems. One approach is to immediately release a statement, apologize as best you can, and lay low until the generally forgetful and always forgiving American public lets it go, often respecting you and your honesty and humility in the bargain. Often the powerful don't have the smarts to heed this advice and instead become arrogant and combative, with disastrous results. For example, if Nixon had gone on television the day after the Watergate arrests and said he was sorry and that it was a mistake by some overzealous people and that it wouldn't happen again, lets move on, that might have been the end of it. Paris could have done it that way and the whole thing could have ended up being dismissed as a titillating invasion of privacy. Or, she could have been outraged, say it was an unforgivable invasion of privacy and attempted blackmail. Or, she could have hammered away until those involved were fined, arrested, or both. Or she could have just played it cute, just two normal young people doing what comes naturally. Truth be told, Paris, her parents, and her advisers didn't know which way to go. So they did nothing and got nothing—no understanding, no sympathy, no endorsements, no money. At least Pamela Anderson and Tommy Lee got a piece of the action from their stolen video. It's rumored that Untitled Entertainment, Paris's management firm, did talk to Guess? jeans about using her in an ad campaign, but negotiations diddled around and dwindled to nothing. Guess? wasn't completely sold on her drawing power, her name familiarity. One of the newer ways to check up on public interest is to check the number of Internet hits a given person has had on Google or other search engine. This approach has a distinct advantage over older polling practices where polsters determined trends through discussion more than actual bean counting. One national survey, in fact, reports that "Paris Hilton" is the most common name people use for making phony deliveries. In other words, Paris does deliver. Yet neither Paris nor Nicky nor anybody else in her family are the most popular Guess? hits on Google; Shana Zadrick, Anna Nicole Smith, and Claudia Schiffer are. But the naughty girl image does suit Guess?, so who knows what the future may bring for Paris.

At the same time, the video may be one of the reasons Nicky has moved away from the Paris party image and toward fashion design. She's not only moved away from swinging blond to subdued brunette, she's signed on with a different management firm, Handprint Entertainment. And there was even talk of her trying to land a spot as a television personality, a move ultimately kyboshed by her father Rick for reasons that no one has quite explained.

The Graham Interview

The video just wouldn't go away. Most recently, in a March 28, 2004, interview of Rick Salomon by London *Daily Mail* columnist

Caroline Graham, we got another summary of the details that anyone south of the Arctic Circle already knew. Obviously still agitated, we're told that the Hilton empire "launched a scathing attack on Salomon. As well as accusing him of purposely leaking the tape." Salomon was alarmed that the Hiltons were claiming he seduced an underage Paris by plying her with whiskey and that she didn't know what was happening, a claim easily refuted just by watching her behavior on the tape. Nonetheless, Salomon sued for slander, and no doubt the interview bolstered his case. It allowed him to reveal the real truth about the tape for the very first time. Here, then, is that truth according to Rick Salomon, as reported to Caroline Graham:

"Paris never wanted this tape out there, but the truth is, neither did I. This was something I made for my own private consumption, and for just a few of my close buddies. People can judge me how they like, but I would like them to judge me on the facts."

Graham cuts away at this point. In spite of playing the victim of the powerful and rich Hiltons, she guesses, the video may be the biggest break in Salomon's life. She goes back to his impoverished childhood in Asbury Park, New Jersey, where, at the age of fifteen, he dropped out of school and made his way to Hollywood. There, he was soon dealing drugs, as he described it, "big time." This meant mixing with the fast young showbiz crowd. The guys gave him money for drugs, the girls gave him sex. That's when he started videotaping his escapades, Paris being just another in a long string of encounters, although in no way does he suggest she was on drugs at the time. Along the way, he married actress Elizabeth Drew, known for doing voice-overs for the *Rugrats* and *Powderpuff Girls* cartoon series, with whom he had two children. He later married Shannon Doherty of *Beverly Hills 90210* fame, and supposedly enjoyed liaisons on the side with such luminaries as Drew Barrymore.

Rick Salomon claims it was well known that he taped his sexual encounters. And Paris knew that when she met him. "When we made the tape," he claims, "I never thought it would be for anyone other that us—or a very tight circle." He also claims that the tape was stored in a safety-deposit box, with a copy hidden in the attic of his Hollywood Hills home. Apparently, his long-time buddy and roommate Don Thrasher stole it and sold it to Marvad in Seattle the same week *The Simple Life* premiered. "I never thought that he would do the dirty on me," Rick bemoaned. "I thought that Don might have copied it and was enjoying it for his own benefit, but it didn't bother me because I trusted him." But their friendship was apparently no match for the allure of big bucks. It was the end of their friendship.

It's no surprise that Rick and Paris would soon encounter each other again in the small, inbred town that is Hollywood, literally spotting each other across a crowded room. At the time, Paris was with the Backstreet Boys' Nick Carter, who may or may not still be her boyfriend. Whenever she goes out now, however, she's on guard, ducking photographers who would love nothing better than getting a shot of her and Rick together. He isn't all that excited about the prospect, of course, seeing how every time she sees him she screams, "Why are you suing me? What is it all about?" He thinks a lot of these public outbursts are for the benefit of her parents. He just wants the whole thing to go away.

Rick Salomon also claims the lawsuits are a legal quagmire. Graham, however, isn't buying his story and still sees him as the hustler he's always been. Otherwise, why did he recently release the complete, full-color version of the tape on his website? "For a man who wished the scandal had never happened," she observes, "he seemed eager to exploit it." He was forced to do it, he counters, because everyone in Hollywood thought he had released the first tape. But the real reason might be that when the Hiltons sued him, he struck back by making a lot of money off the tape by having a Czech company release it—to the tune of $9 million. His latest revelation is that he has twelve more tapes of him and Paris. Ain't show business wonderful?

As for Paris, Caroline Graham reports things are going well. Offers are pouring in, and Bill Stankey, the manager she's hired to handle things, reports, "A sex video would be a train wreck for some people, but it hasn't hurt her at all. In fact, the publicity is helping. She is being swamped with terrific offers."

More Comments on the Video
Drew MacKenzie of the London Mirror:

"The beauty [Paris] has become the butt of endless late-night TV jokes since an internet porn company got hold of a copy of the video she recorded in 2000. Her father Rick has been criticized for letting Paris and her 20-year-old sister Nicky lead a wild party life around the world. Friends of the Hiltons said Rick and his wife Kathy have been trying for years to help Paris overcome her personal problems."

Public relations consultant Dan Klores:

"She's as interesting as Britney Spears that way, and that's not terribly interesting."

Feminist author Camille Paglia:

"She's just nice. She's very niii-iiice—and vulnerable."

Larry Flynt, publisher of Hustler magazine:

"Other than the desire for survival, the strongest single desire we have is for sex."

And sex is the lowest common denominator when it comes to getting the largest number of patrons into movie house seats.

8.

The Simple Life in a Not So Simple Life

The biggest hope for stardom for Paris Hilton to date has been *The Simple Life*, with Nicole Richie. It's the story of two girls from the big city trying to cope with the mysteries of living in a small rural town. A spin-off of the smash sixties cornpone comedy *Green Acres*, itself a spin-off of the earlier, equally corny *Petticoat Junction*, *The Simple Life* had Hilton and Richie milking cows and doing without the chauffeur-driven necessities of their everyday lives to live the life of their fellow Arkansan townsfolk, none of whom seems the least bit willing to wait on the two.

Green Acres had Eddie Albert playing successful New York lawyer Oliver Wendell Douglas (cobbling together a pair of Supreme Court justices' names) who decides to get back to nature by buying a very run-down farm in the sticks. His Hungarian-accented, pampered but sweet wife Lisa, played by Eva Gabor, wants to stay right where they are on Park Avenue and have nothing to do with the move. With his what would be considered today quite sexist theme song lyric "You are my wife," and her retro-resigned "Good-bye, city life," they move anyway. Surprisingly, Lisa comes to love her new life almost immediately—always in full makeup, it seemed, and often decked out in some frilly frock—and it is Oliver who seems to be always bumbling along trying to adapt.

Giving Eva Gabor the role of Lisa Douglas was a stretch for the people at CBS because they didn't think her accent or personality would play well. Martha Hyer, a knock-out blonde known for playing rich girls, was their first choice, but they balked at the $100,000 fee she was already commanding in movies. So they auditioned twenty-six other actresses until Bea Benadaret, a friend of Eva's who was in *Petticoat Junction*, recommended her to producers. Toward the end of May 1965, Eva flew out to Hollywood from New York to audition, practicing the whole way. Producers emerged from the audition stunned, signed her within the hour, saying later they knew Eva was the one because the stage crew kept laughing. For her part, Gabor got two things out of the deal she desperately wanted from Hollywood: stardom and millions of dollars. Paris Hilton should be so lucky to do as well.

And she pretty much has. Generally, *The Simple Life* was well received, and things are looking promising for Paris on the acting front. Television critic Kevin Thompson thought the first episode of the show was well done, stirring up "favorable buzz" (that's showbiz-ese for people talking about you, your show, your performance and saying nothing but good stuff), and he predicted it would be a hit for Fox. He did mention the video and that it might be the reason people were tuning in. After all, he reasoned, the Internet is flooded with it. The video site had the most hits of any sites on the Internet for the week of November 15, 2003. And despite Paris's apologetic withdrawal from the public eye, all bets were that she really loved it, and you can bet Rupert Murdock and Fox did, all that free publicity. They could have put Paris on the air right after the video came out and she would have pulled in huge audiences of the damning and the just plain curious alike. Paris did cancel an appearance on David Letterman right after that, but turned up on the cover of *U.S. Weekly* soon enough. Thompson comforts us by concluding that we need not worry about what the future holds for Paris Hilton. "After all," he says, "the almost insatiable public fascination with the Hilton sisters—especially Paris—refuses to die."

In March 2004, Paris Hilton took a deep breath and, with her dog Tinkerbell in tow, launched the second season of *The Simple Life* with Nicole Richie on location in Miami Beach. This time the girls are crossing the continent in thirty days driving a pink pickup truck pulling a trailer. Now, most grown-ups would be able to make the journey in a week to ten days, but the deal here is that neither Paris nor Nicole has any money, any credit cards, or any boyfriend handy with money and credit cards. And—yikes!—no cell phones. Paris confessed to reporters that she, at the age of twenty-three, had never been on a road trip anywhere, anytime, with anybody. How many people her age can say that? She drives, of course, and she drove a pickup in the first series, but she's never driven a pickup pulling a trailer behind it. And the farthest she's ever driven is from Beverly Hills to Palm Springs down U.S. 15. It was fun, she mused.

To the amazement of many, Paris and Nicole made the first season of *The Simple Life* a hit. Getting up at the crack of dawn—sort of—they performed chores and took odd jobs that they probably never had even heard of. Milking cows afforded them a whole new perspective on the breast; selling hamburgers suggested to them where they could have ended up had their lives not been so blessed financially. The message was that even though the girls are spoiled and coddled, they were open to the new experiences offered by country life and they truly bonded with the people there. Their view of the world may have been narrow to start with but it broadened as time went on.

Part of the girls' humor was scripted for them, but a lot of it was just their own naivete. Paris hated the cows and the barn because of the smell. And she astonished everyone when she said she had no idea that people had to work for a living, that she had never seen a paycheck and didn't know what to do with it. Amazingly enough, Paris and Nicole actually succeeded in baking a pie, and then they accidentally succeeded in letting the dog eat most of it. One of the funniest and most talked about moments was when Paris revealed that she didn't know what Wal-Mart was. A store that sells walls? she ventured. Or things for walls?

In the second season, Hilton and Richie will stay several places as they cross the country, with the same basic concept of fitting in that played so well the first season. It's definitely going to be more interesting and more adventurous because, as Paris says, "Last time, we were just stuck in Arkansas with a family, but this time it's going to be different families every episode." Executive producer Jon Murray says there will be eight episodes this season instead of just four, and they will travel all through the South on their way from Miami Beach to Beverly Hills.

Murray figures Paris and Nicole will again charm television audiences with their innocence and sweetness. He sees them as outlandish, foolish, even clueless, but nice, and always out to have a good time. Their jobs will be arranged for them in advance, but otherwise they're on their own when it comes to most everything else: clothes, hair, makeup, food, fixing the truck, and so on. So it's two leggy blondes against the world once again, and all bets are on the blondes.

Unspoken is the show's supposed anti-rural, anti-Southern bias. While some critics felt the first season's typical farmer came off as a Confederacy-loving, dimwitted fool who somehow managed to come off okay by the final scene, Murray disagrees, saying the show is not about making a social statement but about making people laugh. As Paris Hilton herself has said, "People from the city will be like, 'Oh my God, I cannot believe you did that,' and people from the country think it's funny because they do it every day."

But for Paris Hilton, the show is really all about something else. It is certification that she is indeed an actress, that a national audience can accept her, that the video is not all that they were interested in. The video did change her life and how she sees herself, and she no longer likes going out that much, which is an astonishing change for Paris the Heiress. "It's not that much fun and I really can't even hang out with my friends very much anymore," she has been quoted as saying. Besides, the new series and recording a CD and other actual and potential acting roles will keep her busy at least through 2004. Who knows, she just might turn out to be a really good actress like Elizabeth Taylor or a dazzling personality like Zsa Zsa Gabor. The potential is there to go either direction.

The Nicole Story

When Nicky Hilton decided she didn't want to costar with Paris in *The Simple Life*, Nicole Richie got the part instead. The daughter of singer Lionel Richie, she grew up in Los Angeles with people like the Hilton sisters as friends. She assumed everybody was rich, in fact, and that everybody had more than a passing acquaintance with drugs. She also knew all about scandal, first finding herself defending Paris over the videotape, then defending her godfather, Michael Jackson, over the latest allegations against him. As Caroline Graham reported in the *London Sunday Mail*, by mid-March 2004 Nicole was "suffering a severe case of 'scandal fatigue.'"

People want to know all about Nicole Richie—who she is, where she's from. She was born in Berkeley, California, in September 1981. Her parents, never really a couple, allowed the Richie family to raise her. An exotic combination of races, as Nicole herself has said, "My parents were a mixture. I have French, Spanish, Indian and black [roots]. Even I don't know the whole mixture." She basically grew up pampered and kind of wild.

When Nicky turned down the part in *The Simple Life*, "Paris suggested they should contact me," Nicole reported. "I'd been approached by other reality TV shows, but all they wanted to do was the 'rich bitch' thing—to follow me around shopping. I go shopping, but there's a lot more to me than just flexing a credit card."

And to prove to her father Lionel Richie just how much she wanted to do the show, and how serious she was about doing it, Nicole entered drug rehab almost immediately. It was a breakthrough for her not only professionally but also personally between her father and herself.

9.

Sister Nicky

One of the problems being Paris Hilton's sister is you're always explaining how you're not her carbon copy. You love and admire your sister, naturally, but you still want to be you. Just like Paris hates being called Conrad Hilton's great-granddaughter all the time, Nicky hates being called Paris Hilton's sister all the time. And when Paris started getting a lot of press coverage for doing crazy things, Nicky wasn't necessarily a part of it. So when Nicky changed her hair color from blond to brunette, everybody wondered if it was to distance herself from Paris, especially since the video had just come out. It wasn't. It was because of Melania Knauss, Donald Trump's girlfriend. Nicky was sitting in Bergdorf's salon flipping though *People* magazine when she came across a photograph of Melania and was struck by how wonderful her dark hair looked. So the decision to change color was just that simple. She insists that it is purely coincidental that it happened the same week as the video was released.

In addition to modeling for designers' runway shows and designing handbags for Samantha Thavasa, Nicky Hilton is turning up the heat under her own career. She has signed on with Handprint Entertainment for representation, and she is developing a television show of her own. One of the first gigs she landed through Handprint was hosting a pre-Gold Globes show for the E! network, including a segment on the red carpet with Halston designer Bradley Bayou. Having known her socially for years, he had never seen her in action professionally, and he later said he was struck by her poise as well as her knowledge of fashion. Bayou sees Nicky as being perhaps a bit more mature than Paris, although he lauds Paris for how she manipulates and enhances her public image through notoriety. Nicky's approach is based more on methodically educating herself, something Paris is not known for, and working to achieve her goal rather than employing right-between-your-eyes shock value to garner attention.

The Hilton sisters have collaborated in a number of ways. They share a four-story house in Hollywood that is convenient for each of their professional endeavors, and they have designed a line of jewelry together. There's even talk of a perfume launch, but that's been a bit slower getting off the ground. But Nicky nonetheless is on a very different career path than Paris. She already has two years at New York's Fashion Institute of Technology under her belt, and she has studied at Parsons as well. Now she's in Los Angeles attending the Fashion Institute of Design and Merchandising. While many feel she missed the boat by not doing *The Simple Life*, she just wants to be herself. "I like the complicated life a little more," she has joked. She also has said, "I think it's cheesy for people to be called socialites and live off their family names." Did we hear that right?

10.

What Worries People About Paris Hilton

The thing that secretly worries parents more than Paris Hilton's antics is the impact she is having on young women in their late teens and early twenties. As one commentator observes, Hilton sets the code of conduct for rich young women everywhere. If she can prance, pander, and party, why can't everyone else? Nobody seems to have come up with a credible answer. Just saying it's because Paris is "naughty, tasteless, and embarrassing" doesn't make sense. She doesn't like to be mocked or ridiculed any more than the rest of us, and even though the video was embarrassing it's not all that uncommon in the world of celebrities. In fact, some regard her talking her cell phone call in flagrante as kind of cute.

There are many who admire what Paris has managed to achieve as a model and actress. And while she is proud of being a Hilton, it bothers her that people think she's only riding on the name and not earning her own way. In one sense, you have to admire her for even thinking about earning her own living just because she doesn't have to. Paris Hilton is more than just a hotel in France, more than the center of a universe in which everything is money and everybody panders to those who have it. But getting over that hurdle is going to take time, and it may never happen. After all, for all of her grousing about how much she hates being in the spotlight, she seems to automatically throw herself in it every chance she gets.

Paris Hilton claims that in a few years she'll settle down and get married and have kids. And while we're not sure about the getting married and having kids part, a few more years of maturity couldn't hurt.

11.

Around the World with Paris Hilton

Not only are the Hilton sisters "it" in America and the United Kingdom, they're big in Japan too. They're as famous, in fact, as Kyoko and Mika Kano, some of the most famous women in Japan. And in many ways they are like the Kanos. The Kanos, too, are beautifully packaged, appearing sweet yet sexy at the same time. They first appeared on the Ginza scene, often called Japan's pop culture factory, in 1998, when the Japanese edition of a French magazine ran photos of the sisters in a feature on the most stylish women of 1997. The Japanese public were intrigued and began following the Kanos' every move. The Kanos began turning up everywhere with glitter-dusted cleavage and mouthing their trademark "Young women sob when they see us."

Young Japanese women mimic Kyoko and Mika just as Americans mimic Paris and Nicky. And more sober observers are likewise bewildered as to what the real attraction is, dismissing them as famous just for being famous. Paris and Nicky have it over Kyoto and Mika, however, in terms of money and age (the Kanos are in their mid to late thirties). It's a mystery, as to where the Kanos' money comes from. Kyoko sometimes says it's from shipping, sometimes the stock market. Essentially, she waves the question aside with an enigmatic "Money follows us."

Like the Hiltons, the Kanos' allure is only enhanced by a penchant for designer clothes and shoes, and, unlike the Hiltons, huge diamonds, including Kyoko's 24 carat D-flawless solitaire which she claims is the third-largest round diamond in the world. The press is always poking around looking for some unsavory detail on the two. Who are Kyoko and Mika Kano? they want to know. Where does all their money come from? Some of their fans worry that someday something will surface that will bite the Kanos and stun their fans. "We're 18 karat," Kyoko and Mika insist. "People think we're something cheaper," adding, maddeningly, "We've always had this life, but we find it's important to have a mystery." Other celebrities have held this true—Garbo, for instance. Maybe the Kanos are playing it smart. They're certainly making a lot of money doing it: adolescent girls bought out the entire stock of the Kano sister's lingerie-clad action figure in one day; businessmen pay them $30,000 to show up at their events; rich women pay $250 each to listen to them talk about health food and sexual fulfillment and hawk their trademarked La Busty cream, which they claim lifts the bosom. In the Kanos' case, their breasts are substantial—Mika's G-cup bras are custom-made.

The Kano sisters may soon be in direct competition with the Hiltons as Hollywood continues to look for the next novelty act, let alone the next hot duo. They already have turned down roles in the second Mike Myers *Austin Powers* sequel. Beyond that, they have become notorious in Japan for their open sexuality. Their first book, *Loving*, is a pictorial soft-core daydream of two women in love with each other. "Maybe I'm bisexual," Kyoko teases. "I think it's wrong to live only for men." One American observer of Japanese culture called the attraction similar to combining Pam Anderson with Barbie. And, like the Hiltons, the Kanos never seem to wear the same thing twice. While the Kanos were very nice to the Hilton when they visited Japan, Nicky could help commending that Kyoko's breasts "are like basketballs." For their part, the Kanos, strangers to New York, are hoping to snare front-row seats at the Seventh on Sixth fashion shows in Bryant Park when they finally do visit. "Yeah, right," comments Kathy Hilton. "Like that'll happen."

Paris and Nicky Hilton are the focus of the press elsewhere in the world as well. In New Zealand, the press summarized the sisters' November 2003 visit to neighboring Australia with the clichéd "they were gone from Australia but certainly not forgotten." It was observed that "[d]uring their sensational visit for the Melbourne Cup, the sisters—Nicky, 19, and Paris, 22—did everything expected of two blonde, billionaire, New York celebrities, and more." "Everything" included "skimpy frocks . . . a string of pouting, leggy front-page photographs, and at least one controversial television appearance." There were stories of "late-night debauchery in bars," plus "a fruity liaison with Robert 'Millsy' Mills from *Australian Idol*," although it's not real clear what is meant by "fruity," no doubt nothing to do with horticulture. Finally, one paper described their trip as typical of the Hiltons' elusive fame, "fuelled entirely by a voracious media," ironically failing to get the story straight by first saying that neither sister "has ever had a job" and then reporting they stayed an extra two days in Australia so Paris could model for designer Wayne Cooer.

There is always the competition at home. Alex and Brittany Smith, the "Sheer Blonde Twins," are already appearing in style shows and promoting products. Both are good singers to boot. But the most challenging thing about the twins is that they are all of eighteen years of age.

12.

Lifestyles of the Young and Rich

Who are the rich young contemporaries of Paris Hilton and how do they feel about being who they are? Studies indicate that the suicide rate among this group is significantly higher than among those who are not so fiscally blessed. In the documentary *Born Rich*, which won an award at the 2003 Sundance Film Festival, filmmaker Jamie Johnson, of the Johnson & Johnsons, explored the question of what life is like as a rich kid. His premise was that people basically want to hate people who are rich, and hate them even more if they didn't earn of dime of it themselves. He made the film as a type of therapy because he saw his friends' lives so often turn to disaster. He wanted to know why.

Johnson interviewed ten friends and it seemed that almost none of them were happy, as indicated by how long it took him to get just three of those interviews. Three years. Nobody else in their circle wanted to talk about it. Luke Weil, one of those interviewed, was so unhappy with what he said and how he said it, he sued Johnson to get his interview dropped from the final cut. All those interviewed were disgusted by, and even frightened of, the responsibility involved in having so much money, what one referred to as the "voodoo of inherited wealth." Aside from that, Ivanka Trump fears she can't live up to her parents' expectations, S. I. Newhouse IV prefers living in a dorm room rather than his family's mansion, and Georgina Bloomberg just plain hates her name. All of the interviewees came off as refreshingly honest.

"People have a lot of reservations talking about money in general," said Johnson, assessing those interviewed, "and most kids who are born rich are told from a very early age not to talk about money." Two of the ten who did talk, Trump and Newhouse, did so only because they are personal friends of Jamie Johnson's, which casts a bit of a shadow over how objective the interviews really are.

Born Rich details the bitter divorces, nasty probate battles, and ugly publicity in general that have plagued the Johnson dynasty over the years. There's even a discussion between Jamie and his father, who was involved in a protracted legal tussle over the Johnson estate. His father, uncomfortable talking about money, was against his son making the documentary in the first place, but nonetheless he agreed to appear in it. "There are no courses in college about how to be a hardworking and productive rich person," he later noted. "It's something you've got to figure out for yourself."

Jamie Johnson thought Ivanka Trump came off as poised but was obviously devastated to have heard about her parents' divorce by reading all about it in the *New York Post*. And he thought Stephanie

Ercklentz came off as the poster child for spoiled brats everywhere because she wouldn't stop yapping about the delights of shopping. Being rich is not as easy as those of us who are not rich imagine it is, seems to be the message. Still, it doesn't seem to be a problem for Paris Hilton.

Kevin Thompson, who reviewed the documentary for the *Palm Beach Post*, wrote: "It's obvious the subjects of *Born Rich* want viewers to see them as real people who, like the rest of us, also have real problems. That may be true, but it's hard to be sympathetic when you can practically see the silver spoons spilling out of their mouths."

What's it like being on the

inside looking out?

13.

Inside the Rich Kid's Brain

What's really going on with Paris Hilton, her sister Nicky, and rich people like them?

Seattle Post-Intelligencer columnist Susan Paynter examined this question in her March 3, 2004, column, grouping the strange things rich kids do into several possible categories: impolite, insensitive, not funny, politically unwise, illegal, or downright dangerous. Things Paris has done over the past eight years fall under several of these categories, and the same applies to Nicole Richie and their contemporaries.

Society promulgates rules that must be obeyed, but the rules for the rich are not as rigid as for everybody else, even the famous. For example, Janet Jackson's exposed breast during halftime at the Super Bowl is nothing that can't be seen on most public beaches these days. Ironically, it is certainly less than she's exposed on the jacket of her newest release, *Damita Jo*, which was released right after the incident. Jackson's nipplegate totally eclipsed Paris's video fiasco. Uproar over

Jackson versus snickering over Hilton seems to send the message that it's okay to expose yourself as long as it's not all that public. Yet why can Paris dance basically bottomless on nightclub tabletops and romp basically topless in Vegas hotel swimming pools? It would seem that the rules for the rich are not the same for you, me, and Janet Jackson. Historically speaking, the British aristocracy's guiding principle would seem to apply: Do nothing that will scare the horses.

But we're on the outside looking in. What's it like being on the inside looking out?

Admit it or not, the dominant factor in the lives of the rich is money. For many of them, it's money that someone else has earned and left to them. The classic mantra for the rich in America is that the first generation earns it, the second generation saves it, and the third generation spends it. It almost didn't happen that way with the Hiltons. Conrad wanted not only to earn money, he wanted to give it all away too, but Barron saved him from doing that, and indeed it looks like Paris's generation will be the one to spend it, maybe even giving some of it away in exchange for being loved by the world. Other families like the Hilton's may offer clues as to what the younger Hiltons may eventually do.

Money is rarely spoken about among the rich. Most of us grow up aware of money, concerned about having enough of it, but the rich regard money differently somehow. It's more tied up with their sense of identity as people. Having grown up in luxury, the children of the rich are haunted by anxiety about themselves, their own personal sense of identity in the greater scheme of things, their own personal destinies apart from that of their families. And having a fortune in waiting can wreak havoc on the lives of those waiting for it. Maybe it's the lack of normal emotional give-and-take between parent and child or with other siblings, or the lack of trust among heirs generally, that makes life for children of the rich so difficult. A fortune in waiting can bring out all that is dark in the human psyche. It can breed lust, addiction, greed, hate, revenge, insanity, suicide, even murder. As Seward Johnson, Sr.'s daughter said during the court battle over a half-billion-dollar estate, "This isn't about money. This is about revenge." As well as perversity, it turned out, and incest, greed, and attempted suicide.

Psychoanalyst Melanie Klein thinks we all yearn to return to our mother's womb in one way or another. The womb is a sustained nurturing environment where we are warm, fed, and not disturbed and not threatened. But then we are forced from this safe haven and thrust into an uncertain world where nothing is guaranteed. Some behaviorists have claimed that an heir's coveting of the forebear's fortune is just a yearning to return to the womb. Make that the gold-plated womb.

As easy as life may seem to an outsider, the children of the rich can become alienated from their parents, their friends, and the world in general. Although not spoken about openly, there's reported tension between Paris and her parents because of what her parents refer to enigmatically as "personal problems" that have landed her in counseling programs in Lake Arrowhead, California, Provo, Utah, and London, England.

Famous heirs with personal problems in the past include W. Clement Stone, Charles "Tex" Thornton, and Joseph Hirshhorn—all raised as girls by single divorced mothers. While Averill Harriman's father was authoritarian and aloof, William Randolph Hearst was alienated from his father, and Howard Hughes was orphaned when he was nineteen. Barbara Hutton hated her real father and spent her life looking for a replacement. Peggy Guggenheim had mismatched parents who ignored her, leaving her to be terrorized by governesses. Eleanor Medill "Cissy" Patterson's whole life was scarred by bitterness over her mother and drunken father's disastrous marriage. Mrs. Harold McCormick, the unhappily married daughter of a Rockefeller, saw her children by appointment only. And John D. Rockefeller, Jr., Barbara Hutton, Howard Hughes, several Vanderbilts, and Peggy Guggenheim all remember early years of intense loneliness.

Generations of Vanderbilts, in fact, were plagued by miserable childhoods due to matrimonial catastrophes and their elders' stunted emotional development. Commodore Vanderbilt was as emotionally distant from and brutal toward his own children as his father had been toward him. In the Gilded Age, Alva Vanderbilt wielded absolute control over her children and forced her daughter Consuela to marry the Duke of Marlborough, no great catch, at a cost of $12 million, money the duke was desperate to get his hands on to bolster his family's flagging fortune. In the 1930s, little Gloria Vanderbilt became the pawn in a sensational custody battle between her libertine mother and manipulative aunt. "Every Vanderbilt son has fought with his father," said the third-generation Cornelius II after a long court battle that lost him most of his inheritance.

So, too, Barron Hilton plunged into an eight-year battle to set aside his father's will. Paris and Nicky are rich because of it. But not Conrad and Zsa Zsa's daughter Francesca. Today, she's about as well off as most of the servants who work for people like the Hiltons.

Then there is the bizarre case of the late Seward Johnson, Sr.

Heir to the Johnson & Johnson fortune, at the age of fourteen he was turned over by his mother to one of her woman friends for ten days of training in the ways of sex, initiating him in every imaginable pleasure and technique. His mother took off for England forever to marry a peer, leaving her son in the care of servants. For the rest of his life, Seward pursued only three enduring interests: sailing, breeding cattle, and seducing every female within reach, including his own daughter, Mary Lea, with whom he initiated an incestuous relationship when she was all of eight years old and which continued for the next eleven years, often in the same bed with his wife, her mother. Mary Lea's relationships, needless to say, were ruined for the rest of her life, giving herself over to men as a sex slave, even after becoming successful as a producer on Broadway and in the movies. Money didn't help at either end of her story.

The children of the rich can suffer from severe depression, which may account for the high rate of suicide. Jacqueline Thompson, in *The Very Rich Book*, claims that 80 percent of acknowledged suicides in the United States are among the wealthy. Examples include: Roger Annenberg, twenty-two, son of the founder of *TV Guide*; J. Frederick Byers III, thirty-eight, son-in-law of CBS chairman William Paley; Harvey Firestone III, thirty-two, grandson of the tire company founder; Clifford Heinz II, twenty-six, of the Pittsburgh fifty-seven varieties; and Ethel du Pont Warren, forty-nine, heiress to the chemical fortune and onetime daughter-in-law of Franklin Roosevelt.

The emotional profiles of the founders of these family fortunes in many cases have had a direct effect on the heirs. The founder, usually male, was typically a renegade or a religious adherent or had an obsessive-compulsive personality. Conrad Hilton, as we have seen, was a very religious man who attended mass every Sunday, regularly sought Saint Joseph's guidance in matters of business as well as life, and even met the woman he would eventually marry while in church. Just think, if he hadn't married and later divorced Mary Barron, Paris's great-grandmother might have been Zsa Zsa Gabor.

America traditionally is a nation of renegades, escapees from the established order and traditions of somewhere else. If they could have made it there, they wouldn't have left in the first place. The Guggenheims fled anti-Semitism in Switzerland and ended up peddling wares in the streets of Philadelphia. The Reynolds fled Ireland's impoverished north and started growing tobacco in North Carolina. Sutter's brush with police in his native Germany led him eventually to the California Gold Rush. Gus Hilton left Norway for New Mexico to start a new life tending a general store. It's the renegades who have the ambition and drive to fight for a better life. It's what helped make most of the great fortunes.

As pointed out above, religion often played a part. The pious at one time believed that the accumulation of wealth showed God's smiling favor was upon them—it was the basis for the teachings of John Calvin. In the early 1900s, Russell Herman Conwell, a Baptist minister from Philadelphia, crisscrossed the country preaching his famous "Acres of Diamonds" sermon to capacity crowds. Its message was that going after money was an honorable crusade, a test of one's usefulness to other people and especially to God. And God rewards hard work with hard cash. This philosophy dovetailed neatly with Mary Barron's one-world solution to any problem: prayer. As James Knight, professor of psychiatry at Tulane University's school of medicine, has said, "The promise of protection and power is also found in religion: God promises protection, help . . . provided [you] fulfill certain ethical requirements." That message stayed with Conrad Hilton until his death in 1979, when he tried to leave his fortune to the church.

From an entirely different angle, some psychologists relate control over the rectum with control over the world and therefore the drive to make money, a theory derived from the theories of Freud. "Sigmund Freud . . . maintained that our attitudes and behavior toward money were determined during toilet training, when we established control over the anal sphincter," says Henry Lindgren, professor of psychology at San Francisco State University. "Habits of thrift, Freud said, were derived from the pleasure of retaining the contents of the large intestine." Accordingly, such people often develop three main traits later in life: excessive orderliness, parsimoniousness, and obstinacy. We do know Barron Hilton is stubborn, but we are not privy to his personal habits. And as far as Paris is concerned, don't look for any reflections on Freud any time soon.

Then there is the money itself.

Experts in human behavior say money can bring either happiness or unhappiness, but we're not real clear about what money really is, how it works, and why it affects us so much. Money is like a Rorschach inkblot test, says Arlene Matthews in her book *I Think About Money So Much, Why Can't I Figure It Out?* The meaning, it seems, is in the eye of the beholder. "It intermingles with fantasies, fears and wishes, blending with 'a grab bag full of blind spots, embellishments, denials, distortions and impulses."

Yet talking about money is taboo. People will talk about orgasms, fatal diseases, and ax-murdering cousins before they will talk about money. It lives on the dark side of the soul. As John Cohen wrote in the *Washington City Paper* of March 23, 1990, when an inheritance goes sour "you truly are better off dead. At least that spares you the sight of people clawing through your material world like it was so much carrion, snapping at one another for silver trays and shares of stock."

So what is money, exactly? Is it paper notes or metal coins? Or is it the intangible benefits one can derive from having money, such as food and shelter, protection, social standing, power, and even love? For Paris and her generation, it's being indulged by others because they are rich. And they know it as much as we who indulge them do.

14.

A Paris Hilton You've Never Met Before

The tantalizing question for the twittering press and public alike is, Who is the real Paris Hilton? The mindless party girl falling out of her dress? The blossoming fashion model who knows exactly how to command the catwalk so provocatively? Or the sweetly funny reality show star and budding actress? Donna Freydkin recently reported on the new Paris when she appeared at a Fox luncheon in New York hyping *The Simple Life*. It was held at Oscar's, ironically enough, in the Waldorf-Astoria Hotel, her home turf, but it didn't stop people from staring.

Paris, a quick study in the rules of being a celebrity, showed up three hours late. She looked different than ever before, in a powder blue velour sweat suit, with, one observer noted, pants "perilously low-cut and clinging perched on those narrow boyish hips." She announced that she is a perfectly normal American girl who believes people who demand limos and bodyguards are obnoxious. She does indeed know all about Wal-Mart. And in real life she eats at McDonald's and Taco Bell. That and she always follows her parents' advice to be humble.

This bewildering performance was one of very few since the video surfaced. Mostly she had been hiding out. She was there to promote *The Simple Life* only and talking about the video was not part of the deal, although she did say how embarrassed and sorry about it she was. Needless to say, the comment didn't hurt the subsequent press coverage of this otherwise routine promotional lunch. She told *U.S. Weekly* magazine that she'd been forced into virtual hiding because of the video and she hated it. It had such an impact on her that she was thinking about ways she needs to change her life. And that statement alone could make the parents of a lot of rich kids happy. Maybe.

To many, the renovated Paris Hilton had not changed all that much. A little more bewildered about the world, perhaps, but still the same old Paris. Friends say she is just a saucy young woman who is good on the inside and filled with the kind of soaring dreams many have when they are twenty-three. To those less friendly, she's still too mindlessly arrogant for their taste.

Her wild taste in clothes, being in love with being young and alive, flitting from fun place to fun place, Paris is out to have a good time. And that's a mighty hard sell. Especially when things like the video pop up. Part of Paris's problem there was just being too naïve and letting it happen in the first place.

We are now asked to believe that Paris has matured and wants to be treated as a grown-up. She's had a hard time growing up, we are told, what with the Hilton name and all. Then there were all those schools, including the one for troubled youth in Utah, and the kids who just didn't understand, who wouldn't give her and Nicky a break. As to whether she ever earned a diploma or not, he father won't say. And it probably doesn't matter all that much at the age of twenty-three whether she did or didn't.

Paris Hilton's new life has her going out only to promote her films and then heading home by ten. To the jaw-dropping astonishment of one and all, she says she's thinking serious thoughts these days.

Paris has no plans to work in the family business, and she thinks college would be a waste of time for her because she already knows what she wants in life. First, to act in movies, which will make her father proud, provided they're the right kind of movies. It was one of the reasons she decided to do *The Simple Life*, one of any number of shows she claims she was offered. Her second goal in life is to find the right guy and get married. Kathy had Paris when she was only eighteen years old. At twenty-three, Paris longs to be a mother. "I want to have kids in the next two or three years," she says. "I can't wait to have a little daughter and dress her up."

Is the world ready for a second Paris Hilton?

What more could a girl want?

15.

Buttoning Up Paris for Now

March 2004 was a busy time for Paris Hilton. Sadly, her grandmother died and was laid to rest after a ceremony in Beverly Hills. Paris was also thrown from a horse and kicked at a Tampa, Florida, ranch where she was shooting an episode for *The Simple Life*. Just to be safe, she stayed overnight in the hospital. She thanked people and the press for their concern on the way out the next morning.

Early in April, Paris concluded negotiations to appear in a remake of *House of Wax*. Also, she and Nicole were honored by Altus, Arkansas, when they had a pair of streets named after them: Paris Hilton Boulevard and Nicole Richie Avenue.

What more could a girl want?

END NOTES

CHAPTER ONE: THE WORLD HAS TWO PARTS
People love to hate us... Drew MacKenzie, *The Mirror*, November 13, 2003
It's not my fault... Ibid

CHAPTER TWO: THE BEGINNING OF PARIS HILTON
We would go to parties... *Daily Telegraph*, May 8, 2003
I know that I'm pretty... Drew MacKenzie, *The Mirror*, November 13, 2003

CHAPTER FOUR: FAMOUS FOR BEING FAMOUS
Paris Hilton is famous... Rick Bentley, *Fresno Bee*, December 1, 2003

CHAPTER FIVE: THE PARIS BUZZ: WHO MAKES IT AND WHY?
Anyone in any way... Robyn-Denise Yourse, *Washington Times*, November 10, 2003
When there were only... Booth More and Renee Tawa, *The Record*, November 25, 2003
These girls wanted to go out at night... Ibid
They are pretty, rich, fun... Ibid
I think she's beautiful... Richard Johnson, *The Record*, November 25, 2003

CHAPTER SIX: HILTON FAMILY HISTORY AND WHERE THE MONEY CAME FROM
He always struck me... Zsa Zsa Gabor, *One Lifetime Is Not Enough*, Delacorte Press, New York, 1991

CHAPTER SEVEN: THAT VIDEO
Inconsequential to everything... David Usborne, *The Independent*, November 27, 2003
I feel embarrassed... Ibid
I love my daughter... Ibid
In her debut... Ibid
Paris never wanted... Caroline Graham, *London Daily Mail*, March 28, 2004
When we made... Ibid
I never thought... Ibid
For a man who... Ibid
The beauty [Paris] has become... Drew MacKenzie, *London Mirror*, November 19, 2003

CHAPTER EIGHT: THE SIMPLE LIFE IN A NOT SO SIMPLE LIFE
After all, the almost insatiable... Kevin D. Thompson, *Palm Beach Post*, December 2, 2003
Last time... Adrian Sainz, *AP Online*, March 14, 2004
People from the city... Ibid
It's not that much fun... Ibid
Suffering a severe case... Caroline Graham, *The Sunday Mail*, March 14, 2003
My parents were a mixture... Ibid
Paris suggested... Ibid

CHAPTER NINE: SISTER NICKY
I like the complicated... Charlie Methven, *The Daily Telegraph*, April 9, 2002

CHAPTER ELEVEN: AROUND THE WORLD WITH PARIS HILTON
We're 18 karat... Robert Haskell, *W Magazine*, October 1, 2002
Maybe I'm bisexual... Ibid
Yeah, right... Ibid

CHAPTER 12: LIFESTYLES OF THE YOUNG AND RICH
It's obvious the subjects... Kevin Thompson, *Palm Beach Post*, October 27, 2003
Susan Paynter, *Seattle Post-Intelligencer*, March 3, 2004

This isn't about money... Young-Brueal-Elizabeth, *The Nation*, April 26, 1986

Jacqueline Thompson, *The Very Rich Book*, William Morrow Publishing, New York, New York, 1981

It intermingles with fantasies... Arlene Modica Matthews, *If I Think About Money So Much, Why Can't I Figure It Out?* Summit Books, New York 1991

You are truly better... John Cohen, *Washington City Paper*, March 2, 1990

PHOTO CREDITS

page vii **Paris Hilton**, 2004 Park City - Blender Sessions Rocks With Five Nights Of Music - Day 2, Harry O'sPark City, Utah, United States, January 16, 2004
Photo by Kevin Mazur/WireImage.com

page 3 **Nicky and Paris Hilton**, Stuff Magazine Palms Casino Weekend Keystone Light Pool Party, Skin, Las Vegas, Nevada, United States, August 16, 2003
Photo by Amy Graves/WireImage.com

page 9 **Paris Hilton, Kathy Hilton, Rick Hilton, and Nicky Hilton**, 1987 Mother Daughter Fashion Show, Beverly Hilton Hotel, Beverly Hills, California, United States, March 26, 1987
Photo by Jim Smeal/WireImage.com

page 15 **Paris Hilton**, 2003 Teen Choice Awards - Arrivals, Universal Amphitheatre, Universal City, California, United States, August 2, 2003
Photo by Steve Granitz/WireImage.com

page 23 **Paris Hilton**, voted Best Celebrity DJ, 2004 Dancestar Music Awards - Press Room, Bay Front Park Amphitheater, Miami, Florida, United States, March 9, 2004
Photo by Jemal Countess/WireImage.com

page 29 **Paris Hilton**, FHM Magazine Hosts The "100 Sexiest Women in the World" Party, Raleigh Studios, Hollywood, California, United States, June 5, 2003
Photo by Michael Caulfield/WireImage.com

page 35 **Paris Hilton and Rick Hilton**, Premiere Party for the Simple Life-All Access, Bliss, Los Angeles, California, United States, December 2, 2003 Photo by Ray Mickshaw/WireImage.com

page 45 **Paris Hilton**, The 3rd Annual BET Awards - Arrivals By Galella Ltd, The Kodak Theater, Hollywood, California, United States, June 24, 2003 Photo by Jim Smeal/WireImage.com

page 57 **Paris Hilton and Nicole Richie present the award for Mainstream Top 40 Track of the Year at the 2003 Billboard Music Awards**, The 2003 Billboard Music Awards - Show, MGM Grand, Las Vegas, Nevada, United States, December 10, 2003 Photo by Kevin Mazur/WireImage.com

page 65 **Paris Hilton & Nicky Hilton**, *Heartbreakers* Premiere, El Capitan Theatre, Hollywood, California, USA, March 19, 2001 Photo by Steve Granitz/WireImage.com

page 69 **Paris Hilton**, 2003 MTV Movie Awards - Press Room, Shrine Auditorium, Los Angeles, California, United States, May 31, 2003 Photo by Jeffrey Mayer/WireImage.com

page 73 **Paris Hilton**, Mercedes-Benz Fashion Week Fall 2003 Collections - Lloyd Klein - Runway, Bryant Park, New York City, New York, United States, February 7, 2003 Photo by Jeff Vespa/WireImage.com

page 79 **Paris Hilton**, 2004 Vanity Fair Oscar Party, Mortons, Beverly Hills, California, United States, February 29, 2004 Photo by Barry King/WireImage.com

page 85 **Paris Hilton**, "Wonderland" Premiere hosted by DETAILS + GUESS? - After Party at the New Nightclub Avalon, Avalon, Hollywood, California, United States, September 24, 2003 Photo by Jeff Vespa/WireImage.com

page 95 **Paris Hilton**, 2004 Dancestar Music Awards - Arrivals, Bay Front Park Amphitheater, Miami, Florida, United States, March 9, 2004 Photo by Seth Browarnik/WireImage.com

page 101 **Paris Hilton**, Paris Hilton Co-Hosts "SNL" - After-Party, Ruth's Chris Steak House, New York City, New York, USA, December 7, 2003
Photo by James Devaney/WireImage.com

page 105 **Paris Hilton**, 2003 Teen Choice Awards - Backstage Creations: Day of Show, Universal Amphitheatre, Universal City, California, United States, August 2, 2003
Photo by Mike Guastella/WireImage.com

PHOTO INSERT CREDITS

Paris Hilton and Tinkerbell, FOX Summer 2003 TCA Presentation - "The Simple Life", Renaissance Hotel, Hollywood, California, United States, July 18, 2003
Photo by Ray Mickshaw/WireImage.com

Paris Hilton, 2003 Teen Choice Awards - Arrivals, Universal Amphitheatre, Universal City, California, United States, August 2, 2003
Photo by Jeffrey Mayer/WireImage.com

Paris Hilton and Nicky Hilton, 2004 Vanity Fair Oscar Party, Mortons, Beverly Hills, California, United States, February 29, 2004
Photo by Barry King/WireImage.com

Paris Hilton and Nicole Richie, 2004 Sundance Film Festival - Paris Hilton and Nicole Ritchie Portraits, HP Portrait Studio, Park City, Utah, United States, January 19, 2004
Photo by Jeff Vespa/WireImage.com

Paris Hilton, Motorola 4th Annual Holiday Party - Arrivals, The Lot, Hollywood, California, United States, December 5, 2002
Photo by Jeff Vespa/WireImage.com

Nick Carter and Paris Hilton, The 61st Annual Golden Globe Awards - InStyle/ Warner Bros Golden Globe After Party - Inside, Palm Court at the Beverly Hilton, Beverly Hills, California, USA, January 25, 2004
Photo by George Pimentel/WireImage.com

Paris Hilton, The Palms Casino Resort Celebrates Playboy's 50th Anniversary With Party At Skin Nightclub, The Palms Casino Resort, Las Vegas, Nevada, September 19, 2003
Photo by Denise Truscello/WireImage.com

Paris Hilton, Cartier's Collection Delices de Cartier Party, Cartier Soho, New York City, New York USA, November 14, 2001
Photo by Jeff Vespa/WireImage.com